The Marketing Edge: Overcoming Marketing Challenges to Achieve Peak Performance

Simon Bedros

About the Author

Simon Bedros is a seasoned expert in strategic sales and marketing. He uses his proven track record in marketing and sales to provide real and working marketing strategies to mid-size and big businesses.

Having commenced his career in Telecommunications and marketing he realized that you could have the best products or services in the world, however, if you're unable to sell and market them you can't help people benefit from them.

Simon Bedros is currently the founder of Simon Bedros Consulting Group. A consulting firm aimed at helping clients to establish themselves as the go-to choice in their industry. You can contact Simon Bedros through LinkedIn.

Table of Contents

Chapter 5: Maximizing Customer Engagement

- The importance of customer engagement in marketing
- Developing customer-centric marketing campaigns and strategies
- Best practices for building customer loyalty and retention

Chapter 6: Measuring Marketing Success

- How to measure marketing effectiveness and ROI
- The challenges of measuring intangible benefits like brand awareness and reputation
- Using metrics to inform future marketing efforts

Chapter 7: Managing High-Performing Marketing Teams

- Building and managing a high-performing marketing team
- Hiring, training, and retaining top talent
- The benefits and challenges of outsourcing marketing functions

Chapter 8: Leveraging Technology in Marketing

- The role of technology in modern marketing
- Choosing and implementing marketing automation tools and software
- The potential of emerging technologies like AI and machine learning in marketing

Chapter 9: Staying Ahead of the Competition

- Differentiating your brand in a crowded market

- Innovation and experimentation as key strategies for staying ahead
- Anticipating and adapting to market trends and changes

Chapter 10: Case Studies and Best Practices

- Real-world examples of companies that have overcome marketing challenges and achieved peak performance
- Best practices and insights from successful marketing campaigns and strategies

Chapter 11: The Future of Marketing

- Emerging trends and technologies that will shape the future of marketing
- The evolving role of the marketer in a changing landscape
- Opportunities and challenges for marketers in the years ahead

Conclusion

Introduction

As the world of business becomes increasingly competitive, it's more important than ever for companies to have a strong marketing strategy in place. However, with so many different channels and technologies available, it can be challenging to navigate the ever-changing landscape of modern marketing. That's where "The Marketing Edge: Overcoming Marketing Challenges to Achieve Peak Performance" comes in.

This book is your ultimate guide to achieving marketing success in today's fast-paced and dynamic business world. From building a strong brand to navigating social media, this book covers all the essential elements of effective marketing. You'll learn about the latest marketing trends and technologies, as well as best practices from successful marketing campaigns and strategies.

Through real-world case studies and expert insights, "The Marketing Edge" provides you with the knowledge and tools you need to stay ahead of the curve and achieve peak performance in your marketing efforts. Whether you're a seasoned marketing professional or just starting out, this book will help you overcome common marketing challenges and drive your business to new heights.

So, if you're ready to take your marketing to the next level and gain a competitive edge, "The Marketing Edge" is the book for you. Let's dive in and discover how you can overcome marketing challenges and achieve peak performance!

Chapter 1: The Evolution of Marketing

Marketing has been around for thousands of years, but it has changed significantly since its inception. In this chapter, we will take a closer look at the history of marketing and advertising, the rise of digital marketing, and how it has impacted traditional marketing. We will also explore the changing role of the marketer in a digital world.

A Brief History of Marketing and Advertising

The concept of marketing has been around since ancient civilizations, like Egypt, Greece, and Rome. These civilizations used various methods like verbal persuasion, signs, and symbols to promote their goods and services. During the Middle Ages, street vendors used to cry out to advertise their products, and merchants used trade shows to showcase their products.

Fast forward to the early 20th century, the modern era of marketing began. In the 1920s, mass production and mass communication led to an explosion in advertising. Advertising became an integral part of marketing, with print, radio, and TV ads becoming the norm.

In the 1950s and 1960s, a new era of marketing emerged, known as the "Golden Age" of advertising. This period was characterized by memorable campaigns, like the Marlboro Man and Volkswagen's "Think Small." Advertising became more sophisticated and targeted, with market research playing a key role in creating campaigns.

In the 1970s and 1980s, advertising continued to evolve, with the emergence of new media like cable TV and the personal computer. The 1990s saw the birth of the internet, which revolutionized the way businesses communicate with their customers.

The Rise of Digital Marketing and Its Impact on Traditional Marketing

With the advent of the internet, traditional marketing methods started to lose their effectiveness. The rise of digital marketing brought new opportunities and challenges for marketers. It allowed them to reach a wider audience and measure the effectiveness of their campaigns in real-time.

Digital marketing includes various techniques like email marketing, search engine optimization (SEO), social media marketing, and content marketing. These techniques allow businesses to reach their target audience more effectively and create personalized experiences for them.

One of the significant impacts of digital marketing on traditional marketing is the shift from mass marketing to targeted marketing. Traditional marketing methods like print ads and billboards are still effective, but digital marketing has become a necessity for businesses to stay competitive.

The Changing Role of the Marketer in a Digital World

Digital marketing has changed the role of the marketer in many ways. Marketers now need to be more data-driven and analytical to measure the effectiveness of their campaigns. They need to have a deep understanding of their target audience and be able to create personalized experiences for them.

The rise of marketing automation tools has also made it easier for marketers to automate their campaigns and focus on strategic activities. The role of the marketer has shifted from a creative-focused job to a data-driven and analytical one.

Another significant change in the role of the marketer is the need to be proficient in various digital marketing techniques. Marketers need to have a sound understanding of SEO, social media marketing, email marketing, and content marketing.

In conclusion, the history of marketing has shown us that it is constantly evolving. With the rise of digital marketing, marketers need to adapt and evolve to stay ahead of the competition. The changing role of the marketer in a digital world requires a new set of skills and knowledge. In the next chapter, we will explore the importance of understanding the customer in modern marketing.

Chapter 2: Understanding the Customer

In today's competitive market, understanding the customer is more important than ever before. With the rapid evolution of technology and the internet, customers have more options than ever before, and they are using that power to demand products and services that cater to their specific needs and wants. Therefore, businesses that can gain deep insights into their target audience can build a competitive advantage and achieve long-term success.

This chapter explores the importance of understanding customer needs and behavior and provides detailed guidance on developing buyer personas, customer journeys, and conducting market research and data analysis to inform marketing efforts.

The Importance of Understanding Customer Needs and Behavior

To succeed in today's market, businesses must have a deep understanding of their customers' needs, wants, and preferences. The key to achieving this understanding is to start by listening to your customers. Conducting surveys, hosting focus groups, and using other research methods to get feedback directly from customers is an effective way to learn about their pain points, aspirations, and expectations.

Another way to understand customer behavior is to use data. By collecting and analyzing customer data, businesses can identify patterns and trends that provide valuable insights into customer preferences and behavior. Analyzing data can help businesses answer questions such as:

- Who is my target audience, and what are their interests and behaviors?
- What products or services do they need, and what problems are they trying to solve?
- What are their preferred channels for communication and buying?

Developing Buyer Personas and Customer Journeys

Once businesses have a deep understanding of their customers' needs and behavior, they can develop buyer personas and customer journeys to better target their marketing efforts. Buyer personas are fictional characters that represent the ideal customer for a business. They are built based on data and insights gained from customer research and data analysis. The purpose of a buyer persona is to provide a clear understanding of the target audience, including their pain points, aspirations, and goals.

Customer journeys map out the customer experience from the initial point of contact to the end of the customer's relationship with the brand. A customer journey provides insights into the customer's path to purchase and helps businesses identify touchpoints where they can influence the customer's decision-making process.

To create effective buyer personas and customer journeys, businesses should use a mix of quantitative and qualitative data. Quantitative data includes metrics such as customer demographics and purchasing behavior, while qualitative data includes feedback from surveys and focus groups.

How to Conduct Market Research and Analyze Data to Inform Marketing Efforts

Market research is the process of collecting and analyzing data on market trends, consumer behavior, and competitor activities. It is a critical tool for understanding customer needs and behavior.

To conduct effective market research, businesses should start by defining their research objectives. This includes identifying the questions they want to answer and the data they need to answer those questions. There are several research methods that businesses can use, including surveys, focus groups, and data analysis.

Surveys are a popular way to gather customer feedback. They allow businesses to ask specific questions and get direct feedback from customers. Focus groups are another method of collecting feedback that involves gathering a small group of customers together to discuss their experiences with a product or service.

Data analysis involves using quantitative data to measure the effectiveness of marketing campaigns and identify areas for improvement. Data analysis provides insights into what marketing strategies are working and what strategies are not working. It also allows businesses to identify new opportunities and threats in the market.

Analyzing data is crucial to making informed marketing decisions. By analyzing customer behavior and market trends, businesses can adjust their strategy to better meet customer needs and stay ahead of competitors.

In conclusion, understanding the customer is critical to achieving peak marketing performance. Developing buyer personas, mapping out customer journeys, and conducting market research and data analysis are critical

Chapter 3: Building a Strong Brand

Building a strong brand is crucial to the success of any business. A strong brand not only helps differentiate a business from its competitors but also creates a sense of loyalty and trust among customers. This chapter explores the key elements of building a strong brand, including the role of brand identity in marketing, defining and communicating brand values and positioning, and building a consistent and memorable brand experience.

The Role of Brand Identity in Marketing

Brand identity is the collection of elements that represent a brand. These elements include a brand's name, logo, color palette, typography, imagery, and messaging. Brand identity is an essential component of marketing as it helps to differentiate a business from its competitors and create a unique and memorable impression in the minds of consumers.

For example, consider the Nike swoosh logo. The simple and recognizable logo has become synonymous with the Nike brand and is instantly recognizable. It has become so iconic that the company no longer needs to include its name alongside the logo in advertisements. The Nike swoosh represents the brand's values of athleticism, innovation, and excellence, and has helped to create a powerful emotional connection with its customers.

Defining and Communicating Brand Values and Positioning

Defining brand values and positioning is the foundation for building a strong brand. A brand's values are the core beliefs and principles that guide the company's decision-making and behavior. These values help to shape the brand's identity and influence how it is perceived by consumers.

For example, Patagonia, the outdoor clothing company, has a strong commitment to environmental sustainability. This commitment is reflected in the company's mission statement, which reads, "We're in business to save our home planet." This messaging is reinforced through its products and marketing campaigns, which often focus on the importance of protecting the environment. Patagonia's commitment to sustainability has helped to build a loyal following of environmentally conscious consumers who are willing to pay a premium for its products.

Brand positioning refers to the unique place a brand occupies in the minds of consumers relative to its competitors. Effective brand positioning should be differentiated, relevant, and credible. It should communicate the brand's unique value proposition and what sets it apart from its competitors.

For example, Dollar Shave Club, a subscription-based razor company, has differentiated itself from its competitors by offering high-quality razors at an affordable price. Its messaging is straightforward and humorous, which resonates with its target audience of millennial men. The company's brand positioning has helped it to achieve rapid growth and attract a loyal following.

Building a Consistent and Memorable Brand Experience

A consistent and memorable brand experience is essential to building a strong brand. This means that every touchpoint with the brand, from advertising to customer service, should reflect the brand's values and messaging.

For example, consider the brand experience of Starbucks. From the moment a customer walks into a Starbucks store, they are greeted by the aroma of fresh coffee and the company's signature green and white logo. The store's interior design, menu offerings, and even the language used by baristas reflect the company's values of quality, community, and sustainability. Starbucks has created a consistent and memorable brand experience that has helped to build a loyal following of coffee drinkers worldwide.

Conclusion

Building a strong brand is essential to the success of any business. A strong brand can differentiate a business from its competitors, create a sense of loyalty and trust among customers, and drive growth and profitability. By focusing on key elements such as brand identity, values and positioning, and creating a consistent and memorable brand experience, businesses can create a strong and enduring brand that resonates with its customers.

Chapter 4: Creating Effective Marketing Campaigns

Marketing campaigns are essential for promoting products or services, attracting new customers, and building brand awareness. A well-planned and executed marketing campaign can have a significant impact on a business's success. In this chapter, we will explore the elements of successful marketing campaigns, how to develop creative and impactful marketing messages, and how to choose the right marketing channels for your target audience.

The Elements of Successful Marketing Campaigns

Successful marketing campaigns have a few common elements that help them stand out from the crowd. First, they have a clear goal in mind. Whether it's to increase sales, build brand awareness, or promote a new product or service, a specific goal will guide the entire campaign.

Second, effective marketing campaigns target a specific audience. By understanding the needs and preferences of the target audience, marketers can develop messages and strategies that resonate with them.

Third, successful campaigns are creative and memorable. They stand out from the competition and capture the attention of the audience.

Finally, the best campaigns are measurable. By tracking key metrics such as website traffic, social media engagement, and sales, marketers can evaluate the success of the campaign and make adjustments as needed.

Developing Creative and Impactful Marketing Messages

The messaging of a marketing campaign is crucial to its success. It needs to be clear, concise, and impactful. The following are some tips for developing creative and impactful marketing messages:

1. **Use storytelling**: Telling a story can make a marketing message more engaging and memorable. For example, Airbnb's "Belong Anywhere" campaign tells stories of real people who have used their service to travel and connect with others.

2. **Appeal to emotions**: Emotions drive decision-making, so a message that appeals to emotions is more likely to be effective. For example, Dove's "Real Beauty" campaign appeals to women's emotions by celebrating diverse definitions of beauty.

3. **Use humor**: A funny ad can make a brand more likable and memorable. For example, Old Spice's "The Man Your Man Could Smell Like" campaign used humor to promote its products and went viral.

4. **Be authentic**: Authenticity is crucial to building trust with customers. Messages that feel fake or inauthentic will not resonate with customers. For example, Patagonia's "Don't Buy This Jacket" campaign was authentic and resonated with customers who valued sustainability.

Choosing the Right Marketing Channels for Your Target Audience

Choosing the right marketing channels is critical to reaching the target audience. Here are some examples of marketing channels and how to use them effectively:

1. **Social media**: Social media is an effective channel for reaching a broad audience, building brand awareness, and engaging with customers. For example, Wendy's Twitter account is known for its snarky comments and engaging with customers in a fun way.

2. **Email marketing**: Email marketing is an effective way to nurture leads and build relationships with customers. For example, Airbnb sends personalized emails to users who have viewed or booked a property, providing them with recommendations based on their preferences.

3. **Influencer marketing**: Influencer marketing involves partnering with individuals who have a significant social media following to promote a product or service. For example, Fashion Nova partners with influencers to promote its clothing line.

4. **Content marketing**: Content marketing involves creating and sharing valuable content to attract and engage with a target audience. For example, HubSpot creates blog articles, ebooks, and webinars to educate and attract potential customers.

In conclusion, effective marketing campaigns are critical to a business's success. By targeting a specific audience, developing creative and impactful messaging, and choosing the right marketing channels, businesses can create campaigns that stand out and achieve their goals.

Chapter 5: Maximizing Customer Engagement

In today's highly competitive marketplace, customer engagement has become a crucial aspect of marketing. Engaging with customers not only helps businesses create brand awareness but also helps build customer loyalty and retention. In this chapter, we'll explore the importance of customer engagement, how to develop customer-centric marketing campaigns and strategies, and best practices for building customer loyalty and retention.

The Importance of Customer Engagement in Marketing

Customer engagement refers to the interactions that customers have with a brand. It encompasses all the touchpoints that customers have with a company, including social media, customer service, and advertising. A strong customer engagement strategy can create a positive customer experience, which is critical for building brand loyalty and retention.

One of the main benefits of customer engagement is that it helps businesses build a loyal customer base. Loyal customers are more likely to recommend a brand to others and are more likely to make repeat purchases. Additionally, engaged customers are more likely to provide valuable feedback, which can help businesses improve their products and services.

Developing Customer-Centric Marketing Campaigns and Strategies

To maximize customer engagement, businesses need to develop customer-centric marketing campaigns and strategies. This means putting the customer at the center of all marketing efforts and tailoring campaigns to meet their needs and preferences. Here are some tips for developing customer-centric marketing campaigns and strategies:

1. **Understand Your Customers' Needs and Preferences**: The first step in developing a customer-centric marketing campaign is to understand your customers' needs and preferences. This involves conducting market research to gain insights into your target audience, including their demographics, behavior, and preferences. This information can help you tailor your marketing campaigns to better meet their needs.

2. **Develop Personalized Marketing Messages**: Personalized marketing messages can help businesses connect with customers on a deeper level. By using customer data to create targeted messages, businesses can create a more personalized experience that resonates with customers. For example, a clothing retailer may use data on a customer's purchase history to recommend new items that match their style preferences.

3. **Use the Right Marketing Channels**: To maximize customer engagement, businesses need to use the right marketing channels to reach their target audience. This involves understanding where your customers spend their time online and what channels they prefer for communication. For example, if your target audience is millennials, you may want to focus your marketing efforts on social media platforms like Instagram and Snapchat.

Best Practices for Building Customer Loyalty and Retention

Building customer loyalty and retention is a key component of customer engagement. Here are some best practices for building customer loyalty and retention:

1. **Provide Excellent Customer Service**: Providing excellent customer service is one of the best ways to build customer loyalty and retention. This means responding quickly to customer inquiries and resolving any issues or complaints in a timely manner. For example, Zappos, an online shoe retailer, is known for its exceptional customer service, which includes free shipping and a 365-day return policy.

2. **Reward Customers for Their Loyalty**: Rewarding customers for their loyalty is a great way to build customer retention. This can include offering discounts, loyalty programs, and exclusive offers. For example, Starbucks has a popular loyalty program that rewards customers with free drinks and food items after a certain number of purchases.

3. **Create a Memorable Customer Experience**: Creating a memorable customer experience is critical for building customer loyalty and retention. This means going above and beyond to provide a positive experience that customers will remember. For example, Disney is known for creating a magical experience for its customers, from the music and decorations to the costumes and characters.

In conclusion, customer engagement is an essential aspect of modern marketing. The success of a business relies heavily on how well it can engage its customers and create a positive customer experience. By developing customer-centric marketing campaigns and strategies, businesses can create loyal customers who will recommend their products or services to others and continue to make repeat purchases.

Chapter 6: Measuring Marketing Success

While implementing marketing campaigns is important, it's not enough to ensure business success. It's crucial to measure the effectiveness of these campaigns and determine their return on investment (ROI). In this chapter, we'll delve into the process of measuring marketing effectiveness and ROI explore how to use metrics to inform future marketing efforts and examine the challenges of measuring intangible benefits such as brand awareness and reputation and the ways you can measure these intangible benefits.

How to Measure Marketing Effectiveness and ROI

Measuring marketing effectiveness and ROI is important because it helps businesses determine the impact of their marketing campaigns and justify their marketing spend. Here are some key metrics that businesses can use to measure marketing effectiveness and ROI:

1. **Sales Revenue**: One of the simplest ways to measure marketing success is by tracking the increase in sales revenue. By comparing sales before and after a marketing campaign, businesses can determine the campaign's impact on revenue.

2. **Cost Per Acquisition (CPA)**: CPA is the cost of acquiring a new customer. This metric helps businesses determine the cost-effectiveness of their marketing campaigns. To calculate CPA, businesses need to divide the total cost of the campaign by the number of new customers acquired.

3. **Return on Investment (ROI)**: ROI is a metric that measures the return on investment for a marketing campaign. This metric helps businesses determine the profitability of their campaigns. To calculate ROI, businesses

need to subtract the total cost of the campaign from the revenue generated and divide that number by the total cost of the campaign.

Using Metrics to Inform Future Marketing Efforts

Measuring marketing effectiveness and ROI isn't just about evaluating past campaigns - it's also about using metrics to inform future marketing efforts. By analyzing metrics, businesses can identify areas for improvement and make data-driven decisions. Here are some ways to use metrics to inform future marketing efforts:

1. **A/B Testing**: A/B testing involves testing two different versions of a marketing campaign to determine which one is more effective. By using metrics to evaluate the results of the test, businesses can make data-driven decisions about future campaigns.

2. **Customer Segmentation**: Customer segmentation involves dividing a target audience into smaller groups based on demographics, behavior, and preferences. By using metrics to analyze the behavior of different customer segments, businesses can tailor their marketing campaigns to better meet their needs.

3. **Continuous Improvement**: Measuring marketing effectiveness and ROI is an ongoing process. By continuously tracking metrics and making adjustments to marketing campaigns, businesses can optimize their marketing efforts and achieve better results over time.

Real-Life Examples

To better understand how to measure marketing effectiveness and ROI, let's look at some real-life examples:

Coca-Cola: Coca-Cola's "Share a Coke" campaign, which personalized Coke bottles with people's names, was a huge success. The campaign generated a 5% increase in sales volume in Australia and led to a 7% increase in consumption in the United States. To measure the effectiveness of the campaign, Coca-Cola used metrics such as sales volume, social media engagement, and website traffic. By analyzing these metrics, Coca-Cola was able to determine that the campaign was successful in increasing brand awareness and driving sales.

HubSpot: HubSpot, a software company that provides marketing, sales, and customer service software, uses a variety of metrics to measure the effectiveness of their marketing efforts. One key metric they use is the cost per lead, which measures how much it costs to generate a new lead. By tracking this metric over time, HubSpot is able to determine which marketing channels and campaigns are most effective in generating leads and driving sales.

Nike: Nike's "Dream Crazy" campaign, featuring Colin Kaepernick, generated a lot of buzz and controversy. Despite the controversy, the campaign was a success, generating a 31% increase in online sales and a 17% increase in overall sales. To measure the effectiveness of the campaign, Nike used metrics such as website traffic, social media engagement, and sales data. By analyzing these metrics, Nike was able to determine that the campaign was successful in generating brand awareness and driving sales.

The Challenges of Measuring Intangible Benefits

While measuring metrics like sales revenue and CPA is relatively straightforward, measuring intangible benefits like brand awareness and reputation can be more challenging. However, these intangible benefits are just as important as tangible metrics, as they can have a significant impact on a business's success. These benefits can be difficult to measure because they don't have a clear monetary value. Nonetheless, it is important to find ways to measure these intangible benefits, as they can provide valuable insights into the effectiveness of marketing efforts.

Here are some ways to measure intangible benefits:

1. **Surveys**: Surveys can be a useful tool for measuring intangible benefits like brand awareness and reputation. By asking customers about their perception of a brand, businesses can get a better understanding of how their marketing efforts are impacting their reputation.

2. **Social Media Engagement**: Social media engagement is another way to measure intangible benefits. By tracking likes, shares, and comments on social media, businesses can determine how engaged their audience is with their brand.

3. **Social Media Monitoring**: Social media monitoring can also be a useful tool for measuring intangible benefits. By monitoring social media channels for brand mentions and sentiment, businesses can get a better understanding of how their marketing efforts are impacting brand awareness and reputation.

4. **Website Traffic**: Website traffic can also be used to measure intangible benefits. By tracking the number of visitors to a website, businesses can

determine how effective their marketing campaigns are at driving traffic and increasing brand awareness.

This information can be used to optimize future marketing efforts and maximize ROI.

In conclusion, measuring marketing effectiveness and ROI is a critical aspect of any business strategy. While tangible metrics like sales revenue and CPA are relatively easy to measure, intangible benefits such as brand awareness and reputation can be more challenging to quantify. However, ignoring these intangible benefits can have a significant impact on a business's overall success. Therefore, it's essential to use a combination of metrics and methods such as surveys, social media engagement, and website traffic to measure the effectiveness of marketing campaigns fully. By doing so, businesses can make informed decisions about their future marketing efforts and adjust their strategies to improve their ROI. Ultimately, measuring marketing success is an ongoing process that requires continuous evaluation and adaptation to stay ahead in the ever-changing landscape of marketing.

Chapter 7: Managing High-Performing Marketing Teams

Marketing teams are the backbone of any successful business. They are responsible for developing and executing marketing strategies that help businesses achieve their goals. In this chapter, we'll discuss the process of building and managing a high-performing marketing team, hiring, training, and retaining top talent, and the benefits and challenges of outsourcing marketing functions.

Building and Managing a High-Performing Marketing Team

Building a high-performing marketing team requires a strategic approach. Here are some steps to consider when building and managing a high-performing marketing team:

1. **Define Roles and Responsibilities**: Define the roles and responsibilities of each team member to ensure clarity and accountability.

2. **Set Clear Goals and Objectives**: Set clear goals and objectives for the team to work towards. This will help to keep everyone on the same page and working towards a common goal.

3. **Foster Collaboration**: Encourage collaboration and teamwork among team members. This will help to build trust and increase productivity.

4. **Provide Feedback and Recognition**: Provide regular feedback and recognition to team members. This will help to keep them motivated and engaged.

5. **Invest in Professional Development**: Invest in the professional development of team members to help them grow and develop their skills.

Hiring, Training, and Retaining Top Talent

Hiring, training, and retaining top talent is essential to building a high-performing marketing team. Here are some tips to help you attract and retain top talent:

1. **Define Your Ideal Candidate**: Define the ideal candidate for each role and create a job description that reflects the necessary skills and qualifications.

2. **Conduct Thorough Interviews**: Conduct thorough interviews to ensure that candidates have the necessary skills and experience for the role.

3. **Provide Onboarding and Training**: Provide thorough onboarding and training to new hires to help them get up to speed quickly.

4. **Create a Positive Work Environment**: Create a positive work environment that fosters collaboration, creativity, and innovation.

5. **Offer Competitive Compensation and Benefits**: Offer competitive compensation and benefits to attract and retain top talent.

The Benefits and Challenges of Outsourcing Marketing Functions

Outsourcing marketing functions can be an effective way to reduce costs and improve efficiency. Here are some benefits and challenges of outsourcing marketing functions:

1. **Cost Savings**: Outsourcing marketing functions can be cost-effective, as businesses can avoid the cost of hiring and training in-house staff.

2. **Access to Expertise**: Outsourcing can provide access to a broader range of expertise, skills, and knowledge.

3. **Improved Flexibility**: Outsourcing can provide businesses with greater flexibility, as they can adjust their marketing efforts as needed.

Challenges:

1. **Communication and Coordination**: Communication and coordination can be a challenge when working with an external agency or team.

2. **Quality Control**: Ensuring quality control can be a challenge when outsourcing marketing functions.

3. **Confidentiality and Security**: Maintaining confidentiality and security can be a challenge when outsourcing marketing functions.

Real-Life Examples

To better understand how to build and manage a high-performing marketing team, let's look at some real-life examples:

HubSpot: HubSpot is a marketing software company that has built a highly successful marketing team. They have a team of over 300 marketing professionals who work together to develop and execute marketing strategies. HubSpot fosters a culture of collaboration and teamwork, providing regular feedback and recognition to team members.

Nike: Nike is a global brand that has built a highly successful marketing team. Nike invests heavily in the professional development of their team members, providing ongoing training and development opportunities. Nike also offers competitive compensation and benefits, which helps to attract and retain top talent.

Coca-Cola: Coca-Cola has outsourced some of its marketing functions to external agencies. This has allowed Coca-Cola to access a broader range of expertise and resources than it would have had in-house. By partnering with external agencies, Coca-Cola has been able to develop innovative marketing campaigns that have helped the company stay competitive in the market.

However, outsourcing marketing functions also comes with its own set of challenges. One major challenge is maintaining consistent branding and messaging across different agencies. To overcome this challenge, Coca-Cola has implemented strict guidelines and processes for its external partners to follow. Additionally, communication and collaboration between internal and external teams must be well-coordinated to ensure the success of marketing campaigns.

In order to effectively manage a high-performing marketing team, it is essential to have the right talent in place. This involves attracting top talent, providing ongoing training and development, and implementing retention strategies.

When it comes to hiring, it is important to look beyond just technical skills and experience. Soft skills such as creativity, communication, and adaptability are also important factors to consider. One way to attract top talent is by offering competitive salaries and benefits packages. Additionally, creating a positive company culture that prioritizes employee well-being and work-life balance can help to attract and retain top talent.

Providing ongoing training and development opportunities is also essential to keep a marketing team up-to-date with the latest trends and technologies. This can include attending industry events, providing access to online courses, and facilitating cross-functional training with other teams within the company.

Retention strategies can include offering career development opportunities, promoting from within, and providing a positive work environment that supports employee growth and advancement.

In conclusion, building and managing a high-performing marketing team requires a combination of attracting top talent, providing ongoing training and development, and implementing effective retention strategies. Outsourcing marketing functions can provide access to specialized expertise and resources, but it also requires careful management to maintain consistent branding and messaging. By investing in their marketing teams, businesses can achieve long-term success in the ever-changing world of marketing.

Chapter 8: Leveraging Technology in Marketing

Technology has revolutionized the field of marketing in recent years, offering new and innovative ways to connect with audiences and achieve marketing goals. In this chapter, we'll explore the role of technology in modern marketing, the process of choosing and implementing marketing automation tools and software, and the potential of emerging technologies like AI and machine learning in marketing.

The Role of Technology in Modern Marketing

The emergence of technology has had a significant impact on modern marketing practices. It has enabled businesses to reach wider audiences, personalize their marketing efforts, and measure their effectiveness. Some of the most common technologies used in modern marketing include:

1. **Social Media Platforms**: Social media has become an essential component of modern marketing. Platforms like Facebook, Twitter, and Instagram enable businesses to connect with audiences, build brand awareness, and promote their products or services. For example, the fast-food giant Wendy's used Twitter to create a sassy and humorous online persona, which helped the company to engage with younger audiences and increase brand loyalty.

2. **Email Marketing Tools**: Email marketing tools like Mailchimp and Constant Contact make it easier for businesses to reach their customers with targeted and personalized emails. These tools allow businesses to segment their email lists, automate email campaigns, and measure their success. For example, skincare company Glossier uses email marketing to keep customers engaged with new product launches, exclusive promotions, and personalized recommendations.

3. **Content Management Systems (CMS)**: CMS platforms like WordPress and Drupal allow businesses to create and manage their website content without extensive coding knowledge. These platforms also make it easier to optimize website content for search engines and mobile devices. For example, outdoor retailer REI uses WordPress to create an engaging and informative blog that provides valuable information to customers and drives traffic to their website.

Choosing and Implementing Marketing Automation Tools and Software

When it comes to marketing automation, businesses need to carefully consider their needs and challenges to choose and implement the right tools and software. There are many options available, and each one offers unique features and capabilities that can benefit different aspects of marketing. However, choosing the right tools and software can be a daunting task. Here are some factors to consider when choosing and implementing marketing automation tools and software:

1. **Functionality**: The tools and software you choose should align with your business goals and marketing objectives.

2. **Ease of Use**: The tools and software you choose should be easy to use and require minimal training. User-friendly interfaces and comprehensive documentation can make the implementation process smoother and more efficient.

3. **Integration**: The tools and software you choose should integrate seamlessly with your existing marketing and sales systems.

For example, if your business is struggling to keep track of customer interactions and leads, a CRM tool like Salesforce can help streamline and automate the sales process. This tool can help sales teams manage their customer data, track interactions, and streamline the sales process from start to finish.

Alternatively, if you're looking to automate your email marketing campaigns, platforms like Mailchimp and HubSpot offer powerful email automation features. These platforms allow you to create and automate email campaigns, segment your audience, and track engagement and conversions.

Another important consideration is the level of integration between different marketing tools and software. For instance, if you're using multiple tools to manage your marketing campaigns, it can be beneficial to choose tools that integrate seamlessly with each other to ensure a smooth workflow. Zapier, for example, is great service that seamlessly integrates between different apps and services.

Furthermore, it's essential to consider the scalability and flexibility of the marketing automation tools and software you choose. As your business grows and evolves, you may need to adjust your marketing strategies and tools accordingly. Thus, selecting tools that can adapt to changing needs and accommodate growth is crucial.

Overall, choosing and implementing marketing automation tools and software requires careful consideration of your business's unique needs and challenges. By selecting the right tools, businesses can streamline their marketing efforts, save time and resources, and achieve better results.

The Potential of Emerging Technologies in Marketing

Emerging technologies like AI and machine learning have the potential to revolutionize the field of marketing in the coming years. Here are some ways these technologies could be used in marketing:

Personalization: AI and machine learning can be used to create more personalized and targeted marketing campaigns. For example, AI-powered chatbots can provide personalized recommendations to customers based on their browsing and purchase history.

Predictive Analytics: AI and machine learning can be used to analyze large amounts of data and make predictions about customer behavior and preferences. For example, AI-powered algorithms can predict which customers are most likely to purchase a particular product or service.

Visual Search: Emerging technologies like visual search enable customers to search for products by uploading images instead of typing in search terms. For example, Pinterest's Lens feature uses AI to analyze images and suggest related products and ideas.

One real-life example of a business leveraging AI and machine learning in their marketing is Netflix. By analyzing user data, Netflix is able to offer personalized recommendations and content tailored to each individual viewer. The platform's advanced algorithms analyze user behavior and preferences to recommend new shows and movies, leading to increased engagement and customer satisfaction.

In conclusion, technology has drastically changed the landscape of marketing, offering a wealth of opportunities for businesses to enhance their marketing efforts and reach their target audiences. By choosing and implementing the right marketing automation tools and software and leveraging emerging technologies like AI and machine learning, businesses can gain a competitive edge and effectively engage with their customers in new and innovative ways.

Chapter 9: Staying Ahead of the Competition

In today's crowded marketplace, it can be challenging to differentiate your brand and stand out from the competition. However, there are strategies you can implement to stay ahead of the game and ensure the success of your business. In this chapter, we'll explore three key strategies for staying ahead of the competition: differentiating your brand, innovation and experimentation, and anticipating and adapting to market trends and changes.

Differentiating Your Brand in a Crowded Market

To stand out in a crowded market, it's essential to differentiate your brand from the competition. The first step is to identify what sets your brand apart from others in your industry. This could be your unique value proposition, superior customer service, or innovative products and services.

One effective way to differentiate your brand is by focusing on the customer experience. Providing exceptional customer service and creating a memorable customer experience can set your brand apart from the competition. For instance, the luxury fashion brand Louis Vuitton provides an exceptional in-store experience for its customers, with plush sofas, crystal chandeliers, and personalized attention from sales associates.

Another way to differentiate your brand is to create a unique value proposition (UVP). Your UVP should clearly and concisely communicate the unique benefits that your product or service offers compared to your competitors. For example, Slack's UVP states, "Slack brings team communication and collaboration into one place so you can get more work done, whether you belong to a large enterprise or a small business." By focusing on your UVP, you can communicate how your product or service solves a specific problem or addresses a specific need, setting your brand apart from the competition.

Developing a unique brand voice and visual identity is essential in today's crowded market, where customers have many choices and options. Brands that stand out are those that have a strong and memorable brand identity that resonates with their target audience. Patagonia, the outdoor apparel brand, is an excellent example of a company that has differentiated itself through its brand identity. By emphasizing environmental sustainability and responsible sourcing in its messaging, Patagonia has created a strong and meaningful connection with its target audience.

Consistent branding and design across all touchpoints is crucial for building trust with your audience and reinforcing your brand's identity. This consistency helps customers recognize and remember your brand, which can lead to increased loyalty and repeat business. One example of a brand that has successfully achieved consistency in its branding and design is Coca-Cola. Coca-Cola's logo, red and white color scheme, and messaging have remained consistent throughout the years, allowing the brand to maintain its identity and remain recognizable to customers worldwide.

Innovation and experimentation as key strategies for staying ahead:

Agile Marketing: Agile marketing is a methodology that emphasizes flexibility and adaptability in the face of changing market conditions. Rather than sticking to a rigid marketing plan, agile marketers focus on experimentation, iteration, and constant improvement. For example, Oreo's "Dunk in the Dark" tweet during the 2013 Super Bowl blackout was a spur-of-the-moment response that became a viral sensation and earned the brand widespread praise for its nimble marketing strategy.

Emerging Technologies: Keeping up with emerging technologies is another way to stay ahead of the competition. For example, augmented reality (AR) and virtual reality (VR) are becoming increasingly popular in marketing campaigns, as they offer unique opportunities for immersive and interactive experiences. Brands like IKEA and Sephora have both launched AR apps that allow customers to "try on" furniture and makeup virtually before making a purchase.

Anticipating and Adapting to Market Trends and Changes

Anticipating and adapting to market trends and changes is crucial for staying ahead of the competition. By staying up-to-date with industry news and trends, you can identify emerging opportunities and threats and adapt your business strategy accordingly.

Social Media: Social media is a powerful tool for monitoring and responding to market trends and changes. By keeping an eye on social media conversations and trends, brands can quickly identify emerging issues and opportunities and adapt their marketing strategies accordingly. For example, when the COVID-19 pandemic hit, many brands pivoted their marketing efforts to emphasize safety and social distancing measures.

Market Research: Conducting regular market research is also key to staying ahead of the competition. This research can include customer surveys, focus groups, and competitor analysis.

One example of a company that has successfully adapted to market trends and changes is Netflix. The company began as a DVD rental service but recognized the shift towards online streaming and invested in developing its own original content. This decision has paid off, as Netflix has become a major player in the streaming industry.

Another example is the fast-food chain, McDonald's. The company has adapted to changing consumer preferences by introducing healthier menu options and investing in technology, such as self-order kiosks and mobile ordering. These adaptations have helped the company remain relevant and competitive in the fast-food industry.

In conclusion, staying ahead of the competition requires a combination of strategic differentiation, innovation, and adaptability. By developing a unique value proposition, investing in branding and design, experimenting with new technologies and agile marketing, and staying on top of market trends and changes through social media and market research, brands can stay ahead of the curve and maintain a competitive edge, guaranteeing long-term success.

Chapter 10: Case Studies and Best Practices

Marketing can be a tricky business, and sometimes it takes more than just good intentions and hard work to achieve peak performance. In this chapter, we will explore some real-world examples of companies that have overcome marketing challenges and achieved great success. We will also dive into best practices and insights from successful marketing campaigns and strategies that you can apply to your own marketing efforts.

Case Study: Nike

Nike is one of the most successful brands in the world, but their success wasn't always a sure thing. In the early 1990s, Nike faced a series of public relations disasters that threatened to derail the brand. The company was accused of using sweatshop labor, and there was a backlash against their use of celebrity endorsements. To make matters worse, sales were flat.

Nike realized they needed to make a change, and they turned to their marketing department for help. The marketing team decided to focus on the brand's core values and create a new campaign that would resonate with consumers. The "Just Do It" campaign was born, and it quickly became one of the most successful marketing campaigns of all time.

The "Just Do It" campaign emphasized the brand's values of athleticism, perseverance, and determination. The campaign featured athletes from a variety of sports, including Michael Jordan and Bo Jackson, and the ads were designed to inspire people to be their best selves. The campaign was a huge success, and Nike's sales soared.

Best Practice: Focus on Core Values

Nike's success with the "Just Do It" campaign is a great example of the power of focusing on core values. By emphasizing the brand's values of athleticism, perseverance, and determination, Nike was able to create a powerful emotional connection with consumers. When you're developing your own marketing campaigns, it's important to think about your brand's core values and how you can use them to connect with your audience.

Case Study: Dollar Shave Club

Dollar Shave Club is a company that disrupted the razor industry by offering a subscription service for high-quality razors at an affordable price. When the company launched in 2012, they faced fierce competition from established brands like Gillette and Schick.

To overcome this challenge, Dollar Shave Club decided to take a different approach to marketing. Instead of creating traditional ads, they created a hilarious video that went viral. The video featured the company's founder, Michael Dubin, explaining the benefits of the subscription service in a humorous way.

The video was a huge success, and it helped Dollar Shave Club quickly gain a following. The company now has millions of subscribers and has been acquired by Unilever for $1 billion.

Best Practice: Be Creative

Dollar Shave Club's success is a great reminder that sometimes you need to think outside the box when it comes to marketing. By creating a hilarious video that went viral, the company was able to reach a huge audience and quickly establish themselves as a major player in the razor industry. When you're developing your own marketing campaigns, don't be afraid to be creative and take risks.

Case Study: Airbnb

Airbnb is a company that disrupted the hospitality industry by offering an alternative to traditional hotels. When the company launched in 2008, they faced a lot of skepticism and resistance from established players in the industry.

To overcome this challenge, Airbnb focused on building a strong community of users. The company encouraged hosts to create personalized experiences for their guests, and they used social media to build a sense of community among users.

This approach was hugely successful, and Airbnb quickly became one of the most popular travel platforms in the world. The company now has over 4 million listings in 220 countries and has been valued at over $100 billion.

Best Practice: Build a Community

Airbnb's success is a testament to the power of building a strong community around your brand. From the beginning, Airbnb has focused on creating a sense of belonging and community among its hosts and guests. By leveraging social media and other digital platforms, Airbnb has been able to build a loyal following and drive brand awareness and engagement.

One of the key ways that Airbnb has built its community is by creating a platform that encourages user-generated content. Hosts and guests are encouraged to share their experiences on social media, creating a powerful network effect that drives new users to the platform. Airbnb also hosts regular events and meetups, which give hosts and guests the opportunity to connect in person and build relationships outside of the digital world.

Another important aspect of Airbnb's community-building strategy is its focus on inclusivity and diversity. The company has taken steps to ensure that its platform is accessible to people of all backgrounds and cultures, including offering translation services and providing resources for hosts to accommodate guests with disabilities.

Overall, building a community around your brand is an effective way to drive engagement and build brand loyalty. By creating opportunities for your customers to connect with each other and with your brand, you can foster a sense of belonging and create a powerful network effect that drives growth and success.

Best Practice: Personalize Your Marketing

Personalization is another key best practice that can help drive engagement and build customer loyalty. By tailoring your marketing messages and experiences to the unique needs and preferences of your customers, you can create a more compelling and relevant brand experience that resonates with your target audience.

One company that has excelled at personalizing its marketing is Amazon. By leveraging data and analytics to understand its customers' preferences and behaviors, Amazon is able to deliver highly targeted and relevant product recommendations, advertising messages, and content. This personalized approach has helped Amazon drive customer loyalty and repeat purchases, while also helping to differentiate the brand from competitors.

To personalize your marketing, it's important to invest in data and analytics tools that can help you gain a deeper understanding of your customers. By collecting and analyzing data on customer behavior, preferences, and demographics, you can create targeted campaigns and experiences that are more likely to resonate with your target audience.

Another key aspect of personalizing your marketing is to focus on creating a seamless and consistent customer experience across all touchpoints. This means delivering personalized messages and experiences across email, social media, advertising, and other channels, and ensuring that your messaging and branding are consistent and cohesive.

In conclusion, building a strong community and personalizing your marketing are just two of the many best practices and strategies that can help you achieve peak performance in your marketing efforts. By learning from successful companies like Airbnb and Amazon, and by investing in data and analytics tools, agile marketing techniques, and a deep understanding of your target audience, you can stay ahead of the curve and drive long-term success for your brand.

Chapter 11: The Future of Marketing

The marketing landscape is constantly evolving, and as technology continues to advance, it's important for marketers to stay ahead of the curve. In this chapter, we will explore some of the emerging trends and technologies that will shape the future of marketing, the evolving role of the marketer, and the opportunities and challenges that lie ahead.

Trend 1: Artificial Intelligence and Machine Learning

Artificial intelligence (AI) and machine learning are quickly becoming essential tools in the marketer's toolkit. AI-powered marketing automation allows for more targeted and personalized messaging to consumers. For example, Netflix uses AI to recommend shows and movies to users based on their viewing history, while Amazon uses machine learning to suggest products based on a user's browsing and purchasing history.

Trend 2: Voice Search Optimization

With the rise of smart speakers and voice assistants, voice search is quickly becoming a key player in the search engine optimization (SEO) game. Marketers will need to optimize their content for voice search queries to ensure they are visible to consumers who are using voice search. For example, if someone asks their smart speaker for recommendations on the best restaurants in a certain area, businesses that have optimized their content for voice search are more likely to be recommended.

Trend 3: Virtual and Augmented Reality

Virtual and augmented reality (VR/AR) have already started to make an impact in marketing, and it's likely that this trend will continue to grow in the coming years. Brands can use VR/AR to provide immersive experiences for consumers, such as allowing them to try on clothing or see how furniture would look in their home. For example, IKEA's Place app allows users to see how furniture would look in their space using augmented reality.

Trend 4: Social Media Commerce

Social media has become a major player in the world of e-commerce, and it's likely that this trend will continue to grow. Many social media platforms, such as Instagram and Facebook, now allow businesses to set up shop directly on their platform, making it easier for consumers to purchase products without ever leaving the app. For example, Glossier has built a thriving business by selling their skincare and makeup products directly on Instagram.

Trend 5: Personalization

Consumers are increasingly expecting personalized experiences from the brands they interact with. Marketers will need to use data and technology to create tailored experiences for their customers. For example, Spotify uses data on users' listening habits to create personalized playlists and recommendations.

The Evolving Role of the Marketer

As technology continues to advance, the role of the marketer will also continue to evolve. Marketers will need to become more data-driven and analytical, using technology to measure the effectiveness of their campaigns and make data-driven decisions. However, creativity will remain a critical skill for marketers, as they will need to find new and innovative ways to reach consumers.

Opportunities and Challenges for Marketers

The future of marketing presents both opportunities and challenges for marketers. On one hand, technology allows for more targeted and personalized messaging, creating the potential for higher conversion rates and increased ROI (return on investment). On the other hand, consumers are increasingly wary of intrusive advertising and are seeking more authentic and transparent interactions with brands. Marketers will need to find a balance between personalization and respect for privacy, and focus on building authentic relationships with their customers.

In conclusion, the future of marketing is exciting and full of potential. Marketers who are able to stay ahead of the curve and adapt to the changing landscape will be the ones who achieve success in the years to come. By embracing emerging technologies, staying data-driven and analytical, and focusing on building authentic relationships with their customers, marketers can ensure that their brand remains relevant and successful in the future.

Conclusion

While we come to the end of this book, the journey of marketing is far from over. The world of marketing is constantly changing and evolving, challenging marketers to think creatively and adapt to new trends and technologies. The Marketing Edge: Overcoming Marketing Challenges to Achieve Peak Performance has explored the challenges and opportunities that marketers face today, providing strategies and tactics that can help marketers succeed in a dynamic and ever-changing market.

Throughout this book, we have seen how successful marketing campaigns are built on a foundation of market research, consumer insights, and a deep understanding of audience behavior. We have explored the importance of developing a unique value proposition, investing in brand identity and design, building communities, and utilizing data and analytics to make informed decisions.

As we look to the future, emerging technologies and trends will continue to shape the marketing landscape. Artificial intelligence and automation are becoming more prevalent, and sustainability and social responsibility are becoming increasingly important to consumers. Marketers must stay vigilant and adaptable to these changes, leveraging new technologies and trends to connect with people in a meaningful way.

At the heart of successful marketing is the ability to connect with people in a genuine and authentic way. By understanding the values, motivations, and desires of your audience, you can build trust and create long-lasting relationships. The Marketing Edge is about achieving peak performance with integrity and empathy for the people you are trying to reach.

In conclusion, The Marketing Edge has provided a comprehensive guide for marketers looking to overcome challenges and achieve success in today's dynamic marketplace. By combining strategic differentiation, innovation, and adaptability, marketers can stay ahead of the curve and maintain a competitive edge. We hope that the insights, best practices, and real-world examples in this book inspire you to take your marketing efforts to the next level and achieve peak performance. Remember, success in marketing is not just about achieving your goals, but doing so with a deep understanding and respect for your audience.

www.ingramcontent.com/pod-product-compliance
Lightning Source LLC
Chambersburg PA
CBHW071115220526

45467CB00004B/1878